T0149238

LIGHTNING
WITHOUT
THUNDER
IS LIKE

Joy

UNSPEAKABLE

LIGHTNING
WITHOUT
THUNDER
IS LIKE

Joy

UNSPEAKABLE

Evelyn Cowan

LIGHTNING WITHOUT THUNDER
IS LIKE JOY UNSPEAKABLE

iUniverse books may be ordered through booksellers or by contacting:

iUniverse
1663 Liberty Drive
Bloomington, IN 47403
www.iuniverse.com
844-349-9409

ISBN: 978-1-6632-0900-9 (sc)
ISBN: 978-1-6632-0901-6 (e)

Print information available on the last page.

iUniverse rev. date: 09/29/2020

Dedicated to my beautiful
Granddaughter, Aaliyah,
The sweetest thing this side of heaven
whom I adore, more and more

Contents

Midnight Prayer

Angel of God, here so near to protect,
Guide me and guard me
And enfold me in your wings.
And shelter me from any harm
That this earthly life brings.
For God knows that from my birth,
I am a stranger and sojourner
Here on this earth.
So, be ever with me as I solemnly roam,
Til I finally reach my heavenly home.
For death is but a new beginning,
Or so it would seem.
And merrily, merrily, merrily
Life is but a dream.

Analogy of Life

Life is like a most cherished music box.
You wind it up, and it begins to play
An enchanted melody, over and over again.
But it gets slower and slower
Towards the end,
Until eventually it stops…mid song.

Ode to India

Death is to go skipping and laughing
Into eternity, unburdened and unafraid.
Which, for one more day of life on earth,
You would never endeavor to trade.
It is to all but forget the months of weeping
And call to sweet remembrance
All the seasons of reaping.
While angels play with your hair
As you lie sleeping.
And, with no debts to repay,
You swear to take to your grave
All the untold secrets of the universe
That you have been keeping.

Revival

I nearly passed away this past winter,
When the flowers faded,
The grass withered,
And the leaves turned to brown.
But miraculously, by spring time,
I was once again, flourishing,
Like the green grass, the rosebuds,
And my awesome faith, new found.

Sometimes I Feel Like A Motherless Child

Have you ever heard the unrelenting cry
Of a motherless child?
Wanting nothing more than her mother's
Sweet and delicate smile.
Like a beautiful flower
Clinging to the earth,
But ever reaching for the sun,
And growing wild.
Secretly desiring the shadow
Because she is not comforted
In the manner so mild.
She can scarcely remember
The warmth and tenderness
Which she possessed for awhile.
Such is the unanswered prayer of despair
Of a motherless child.

Spirit Filled

Thank you, Father, for your Holy Spirit
Which surrounds me, astounds me,
Indwells me, compels me.
Which directs me, protects me.
So I don't have to cry no more.
And I won't have to die no more.

Compensation

Unlike those that be slain by the sword,
I shall go from my labour
To my sweet reward.
And enter into God's blest rest.
For the Lord hath bid his guests.

How Sweet the Sound

Grandma, on this holy day, 38 years ago,
You hung your head and died.
Escaping from all the pain and affliction
Of the abominable heathen, in their pride.
But I know of a certainty,
That you are still my guide.
Continue to speak to me, Grandma.
Continue to speak through me, Grandma.
For it is amazing grace
That saved a soul like me.
I was lost, but now I'm found.
Was bound, but now I'm free.
Thank you, my sweet Jesus,
That I no longer have to dwell in hell.
But I shall abide down by the riverside,
Where I've laid down my burden.
God bless my soul!
For I've finally reached my goal.

Fearless Faith

I fear nothing but Almighty God.
I don't even fear death.
Because, what a joyous reunion it will be
When I reach my final destiny.
My faithful friends on earth
Are precious few, but true.
Yet, love them as I do,
My countless saints in light,
Dwelling in a land where there is no night,
Are infinite as their teardrops of joy
Filling the ocean blue.

Strength for the Journey

Heavenly Father,
Please continue to increase my stamina
As you strengthen and lengthen my days.
And, for the perfect peace of God,
I give thee all the praise.
Father, please keep me always
In thy constant care.
And continue to bless me
With peace beyond compare.

Message to my Aaliyah

Almighty God hath planted me here
Within this sacred place.
And sheltered me, and saved me
By His glorious grace.
But the unshakable, unbreakable bond
That exists between me and thee
Spans beyond all time and space.
My prayers and blessings are ever with you.
With God, I have conferred.
So, rest assured in the knowledge
That you are, now and forever
Sheltered by the Good Shepherd.

Gratitude

I feel so satisfied
In the silences of my soul.
So content, so fully fulfilled, so consoled.
I am so grateful to my God
For my gifts and anointing.
Even the pleas and prayers
Of departed saints, which were of old.

Reveal thy Will

Let it rain.
Let it pour.
Let it thunder.
Let it roar.
Reveal thy will, O God.

Solemn Prayer

Heavenly Father,
Thank you for ordaining me,
Even for anointing and appointing me
A prophetess, poetess and a priestess
Unto the nations.
And, thank you for delivering me from evil,
And leading me not into temptation.
Amen. And. Amen. And. Again, Amen.

Reflection

The sweet taste of freedom
Is like honey to my mouth.
How I love the sound of
The passing train.
How I love the sound of
The falling rain.
How I love the song of the South.
And, may I always remain
Part of its refrain.
For my God hath redeemed me
From the insufferable pit.
And this is my rest for evermore
For I have desired it.

Spiritual Splendour

When I was in bondage,
Deep within the doldrums of despair,
I would lie in bed, and picture myself
In my sacred sanctuary in Scarborough Faire.
And, in my mind, I was there.
Now, through the tender mercy of my God,
My dreams have come true to life,
And I am finally here.
Now I have new dreams to dream.
And, envision them, If I so dare.
For it is a mighty merciful God
Who hears and answers prayer.

Bound for Glory

For the weary traveler,
There's a train a comin'.
Ask not for whom the whistle blows,
It blows for thee,
Just as sure as the river flows
Into the boundless sea.
I've got my ticket.
I've paid my fare.
And can't hardly wait
Til I get there.
As I was about to embark
The mighty thunder roared.
And the Lord, himself. Stretched forth His hand,
As he sounded the command, "All aboard."

Spiritual Warfare

One life is filled with miracles and magic.
While others are nothing less than tragic.
The difference is God.
Just as He blesses me in everything
That I put mine hand unto,
So do curses await those
To whom they are due.
By mine own mother, I was evicted.
By mine own daughter, I was greatly afflicted.
But we are all now reaping what we've sown.
And the greatest blessings came
After I was disowned.
I am no longer afflicted.
Yet they are both addicted,
Having sold their souls to sin.
I have begged and pleaded in vain,
For them to repent, and begin again.
And enter into the portals of peace,
Where sorrow and sighing finally cease.
Because Jesus can soothe your soul,
Just as He does mine.
And, you, too can slowly rise,
Leaving sin and death behind.

Bliss

I awakened one glorious morning,
And thought I was in heaven.
I had plenty to eat.
And an exalted throne
For the soles of my feet.
Although Satan hath desired to have me,
That he might sift me as wheat.
But, thus I remain, since my rebirth.
And shall continue to dwell
As the days of heaven upon the earth.

Winter In Georgia

Happiness is being in my sanctuary
Listening to the gentle rain
Dance upon the roof of my trailer.
Without a single care nary.
And here I shall remain til I die,
Should Jesus tarry.

Home at Last

I dwell in a quaint, haunted trailer.
And it is my very own sacred sanctuary,
Wherein, therein, I've found prefect peace.
And I could not ask for better bliss than this.
A place to call my own,
A place to call home.
Never again to roam.
It shields me from all the former
Heartache, affliction, and strife.
And I shall abide,
With holy angels at my side,
Within these walls, all the days of my life.

A Goodly Heritage

There is an infinite line that exists
Between my matriarchs and me.
I looked high and still could not see them,
So I climbed our ancestral tree.
How I long to abide with Mary, Patience,
And all the rest.
But I must needs wait until I enter
Into God's blest rest.

The Power of a Praying Grandmother

Although she may be long gone
My Grandma's prayers are
Yet sustaining me.
And, like a never ending song.
So, thus, will I pray for
My precious Aaliyah fervently.

Generations of Execration

From my early childhood,
I experienced abominable execration
At the hands of my mother.
Unbearable heartache and grief
Unlike any other.
Then, after I gave birth to a daughter,
She was ripped from my loving arms,
And endured unbearable, irreparable harm
By a cruel, cold system which laid claim to her
Because I was left homeless and alone.
Then, when my evil mother took custody of her,
I went from helpless to hopeless.
In addition, we were both fatherless.
But I had the immense and immeasurable
Love of my Grandma, my saving grace.
Today, my daughter also has a lovely daughter,
Who, truly, is my joy and crown.
But, to my sheer horror, her mother
Has descended to the nether parts of the earth,
And become the most miserable, wretched
Whore in town.
And the execration has been passed down.
I was forced to leave my granddaughter
When I unwillingly fled for my life
To dwell here in perfect peace.
And still, the execration has not ceased.
But, thankfully, it skips a generation.

My precious child, Grandma will be here,
Waiting in the wings to receive you
When you come of age.
And, you too, can escape like a bound bird
Released from its cage.
Just as my beloved Grandma is waiting,
In her heavenly mansion to redeem me,
I shall, like an ensign, stand upon my watch,
Waiting, with open arms, to welcome thee.

For Doris

My dearest frienemy,
You lived for but a moment in time.
Not sixty seconds, but sixty years.
When God reached down and
Delivered you from all your fears.
And wiped away all of your untold tears.

Silent Prayer

Heavenly Father,
Thank you for hearing my silent cries.
Thank you for manifold miracles
Manifested before mine eyes.
For mine eyes have seen the glory
Of the coming of the Lord.
Thank you, my Lord, for all of the blessings.
O, how great the sum.
Infinite, innumerable, immeasurable.
Which were, and art and art to come. Amen.

Fallen Angel

My beloved daughter,
How I was crushed with the realization
That you had sold your soul to sin.
How it utterly broke me when I considered
What might have been.
But God hath made you a new creation.
And, today, that is cause for celebration.
Your old self is forever gone.
Awake, my child, to a brand new dawn.
Because you have empowered
By the Holy Spirit, and you are now
Clothed in Christ's righteousness.
And, in spite of your past woundedness,
You are God's divine masterpiece.
May my mistakes not hinder you,
But God's grace always guide you through.
This is my heartfelt prayer for you
May you inherit the blessings
Of your ancestors before you.
Your father visits me often in my dreams,
And wants you to know he will always adore you
Even more so than you could ever gleam.
For tomorrow is not promised.
It is merely a dream.
So, go! Conquer your fears, and thrive.
And possess paradise while you are still alive.

Still Waters Run Deep

I am on a spiritual journey.
Measured not in miles, but milestones.
It's like I fell asleep on a raft,
Completely unmindful of my sojourn.
But, by the time that I awakened,
I'd drifted so far down the river,
I was past the point of no return.
It was like the calm
In the midst of the storm.
Like how the ever sustaining sun
So radiantly keeps you warm.
And my soul rested in peace
In the very moment when
All of my doubts and fears ceased.
And the Holy Spirit rocked me back to sleep.
And I inherited peace like the river,
Because still waters run deep.

Slowly I Rise

My God is working in me mightily.
Illuminating His divine glory for all to see.
Like an ever-so-gentle, steady rainfall
Softening the furrows of the unquenched earth,
He has validated and confirmed
My mystifying and exalted worth.
Like a lifetime, measured in the span
Of all of the selfless sacrifices
Of a departed saint, who nevermore dies,
In the beauties of holiness,
From the womb of the morning,
Slowly I rise.

Lightening without Thunder
is like Joy Unspeakable

I am so fully fulfilled.
My cup runneth over.
And I delight myself in joy unspeakable.
Like the showers of blessing
That come with the morning.
Like the magical miracles
That come with no warning.
And I must take a moment
To catch my breath
After being visited by angels
Because love is strong as death.
Thus, my joy is unspeakable,
Like the entrapped song of the mute.
As I am enticed to partake
Of the fresh forbidden fruit.

Obituary

I was born in Georgia, and I shall die here.
But my spirit shall return with the spring,
As my laughter resounds upon the wind's wing.
With the sacred song of the sparrow,
My joyful soul shall sing.
For here is all that I hold most dear.
So, when I cast my burden down
At the feet of the King,
I'll adorn my white robe and my crown.
Because I have trodden the path so narrow.
With one voice, let all the saints ring.

A Prayer for my Beloved

Heavenly Father,
Please bless my most precious Aaliyah,
And keep her in your constant care.
I have placed her in your
Mighty, protective, loving hands,
And I shall keep there.
So, Father,
Please keep my beloved
From any harm, from any pain.
For I've placed her in your hands, Lord,
And there she shall remain. Amen. And Amen.

For Sister Pat

Faithful woman of God,
You serve mankind with bands of love,
With inspiration and guidance
Sent straight from above.
With timeless, tireless devotion and zeal,
You teach, you preach, you soothe and heal.
May God bless you in all that you do,
In everything that you can put your hand unto.
Vow taking, cooking baking, smile making
Wise and wonderful you.
You are a saint for all seasons.
And I truly adore you
For all of these reasons.
May all the love you give
Be returned unto you a hundredfold.
For God's love shines through you
In countless ways untold.

For Angel

How I have missed you
Over the past five years.
I have faced your fears,
And I have cried your tears.
Because you will always be
A precious part of me.
For you I pray all the day,
Knowing that Almighty God hears.
Be strong, my child,
For you shall prevail.
And trust in God
Because He will never fail.
I will keep on loving you
More and more and more.
Because you are my child,
And you're worth fighting for.

Delivered from Evil

The Lord hath brought me out of bondage
With a mighty, mighty strong hand.
Through the parched wilderness,
And into the Promised Land.
And I guess I will never understand
Why my own mother could
Cast me out to die.
Why she despises me
Shall always remain a mystery.
Because I know that I cannot undo history.
She made me to walk through the fire.
But my Almighty God hath exalted me
To keep soaring higher and higher.
And, because He raises me up,
I jubilantly send the praises up.
And I shall until I face inevitable death…
Until I take my very last breath.
When my chain gets too heavy to bear,
I will depart this world without a care.
So, from here on out, from this very night,
I'll just keep right on walking towards the light.
And I shall see her no more
To whom I was borne,
That stranger I called my mother.
No, not in this life, nor any other.

Now I Lay Me Down to Sleep

Now that I've reached the ripe age of 64,
I look back on my life,
With all of its up and downs.
And, in the secrets of my contented soul,
I reflect upon all the blessings of old.
How I have been a partaker
Of life's overflowing cup.
How I have been privileged to sit
At the Lord's table, and sup.
I've received endless miracles, as He hath
Carried me from glory to glory.
And now, I've reached the final chapter
Of my amazing story.
And I've known love,
Precious and pure, sent from above.
I've entertained angels from on high
Who shall carry me to heaven on eagle's wings
When my time draws nigh.
And, by and by, I'll exhale my final breath,
And triumphally die.
But not until I have given to this ol' world
All that I have to give.
But, for now, I think I will bring out my good silverware,
And let down my lovely silver hair,
To celebrate a life well lived.

For Earl W.

As you look to the sky,
And ask God why, oh why
Your beloved son had to die,
Remember that sometimes God's mysteries
Are beyond our human comprehension.
But let me not fail to mention
That although you parted ways
At the river's edge,
Which left you feeling
Like you were standing on a ledge,
In God's eternal presence
He will forever abide.
And, he shall greet you again
On the other side.